FURTHER AFIELD

With a Camera

For Mum,
with all my love

FURTHER AFIELD
With a Camera

POLLY PULLAR

Langford Press

Langford Press
Book Corner,
2 High Street, Wigtown,
Wigtownshire, DG8 9HQ
Tel: 01988 402400
Fax: 01988 402010
www.langford-press.co.uk
Email sales@langford-press.co.uk

Graphic design by Freddy Pullar
Technical layout by David Hilditch
Typeset in Goudy Old Style & Garamond
Printed and bound in Singapore
under the supervision of
MRM Graphics Ltd, Winslow, Bucks, UK.

A CIP Record for this book is available
from the British Library
ISBN: 1-904078-10-9

With special thanks to David Hilditch, Keith Brockie, Anna Price,
and MRM Graphics Ltd for the Origination and Proofing.

Introduction

I have always been fortunate to live in the most inspirational places. When I was still at a very impressionable age, my family moved to Britain's most westerly mainland peninsular, Ardnamurchan. In this beautiful remote location, my passion for the west coast of Scotland came to the fore. Here my total adoration of wildlife, wild places, the sea and Scotland's dramatic light, became all-consuming, and since that time, I have found that there are simply not enough hours in the day to further my love for endeavouring to capture this on film.

At the age of 8, an aunt gave me my first camera – a Kodak Instamatic 33, which must have cost my parents a fortune as I burned up film at a frightening rate taking endless pictures of our huge menagerie. I have always been surrounded by animals. My mother would probably deny that much of this was due to her own love of the furred and feathered, but with or without her influence, my love for birds and beasts has always known no bounds. That first camera was the beginning and our animals were my first models. Early albums show dreadful pictures of dogs and cats posed on rocks in the garden which bordered the Sound of Mull, and *family snaps* of everyone in awkward poses. My second camera took me up several stages. This was a superb large, cumbersome Nikkormat – a sturdy 35mm camera with several really good lenses that was kindly lent to me by my stepfather as I was leaving to spend part of the summer holidays with my small cousins. The next portraits that emerged were certainly an improvement on the early pictures, but perhaps much of that was due to the fact that my little cousins overflowed with character, loved modelling, and posed quite shamelessly.

I had wanted to become a vet since I was about three years old. However, by this stage my academic prowess proved that I was certainly not going to make the grade. But at Gordonstoun I found myself taking most of the pictures for the school magazine, and loved developing my own black and white pictures which the school encouraged me to do at every opportunity. Now I thought I would like to be a photographer and writer, and intended to aim for that instead. However, failure to secure a maths O'level put paid to photography college, and while I wasted months and months trying unsuccessfully to get one, I now realise that I could have been doing other much more worthwhile things. Modern educationalists have a great deal to answer for – surely it is far more preferable, and should in fact be a rule, that teachers encourage children in the subjects in which they excel and not those for which they clearly have no aptitude.

Before marrying and taking up farming once again, I had my own photographic business specialising in children and animal's portraiture, mostly in black and white. There were also weddings which I hated as they were extremely nerve-wracking, and my lack of technical ability, particularly with flash, was always a worry. I gave up before I made a total nonsense of things. After all you can hardly ring up next day and say, "would you mind if we took those pictures again next week?"

Now my picture taking is sadly sporadic. But first and foremost I am a mother, something which brings me ultimate joy. I have also surrounded myself with so many animals that getting away from home is very difficult, and the pictures in this book have been taken during the limited amount of time I spend with my camera. Obviously some of our animals and birds are my subjects, and many of the pictures in this book have been taken very close by. I have always used Nikon equipment: an FM2, and more recently an F90X, with 24mm, 50mm, 105 micro, 180mm and 300mm lenses. Once my son Freddy has left home, I intend to fill the void with more photography, and would like to venture over to the western isles far more frequently, because it is here that my heart will always lie. The unique photographic opportunities there are always fraught with difficulties. For example, you will find some of the most stunning flora in the British Isles, yet the photographer is frequently hampered by lack of light, or wind so strong that the flowers dance a Highland Fling – in short, impossible conditions for the camera. But it is these very qualities that make Scotland's wild places so magnificent.

Living with a creative soul is awkward and hard to contend with. On the most magical days of the year I frequently find myself with visitors, prior engagements, other work, or simply day-to-day problems. And it is very hard on these occasions not to become extremely frustrated. Sometimes too, it is hard for other people to understand the creative mind. The pictures in *Further Afield*, hopefully represent just a few of the moments that I have managed to capture between times. That my 15 year old son has completed the book's design with me, and that we are still speaking to one another after this, is to me a great reward, and I think his achievement is wonderful. I think you will detect a huge passion for the natural world; for trees, flowers and landscapes, domestic and wild animals, and of course sheep and goats which definitely play a very important role in this book. *Further Afield*, is an appetiser for what I would like to do far more of in the future.

Polly Pullar, Aberfeldy, 2003

Foreword

It is said that successful photographs of animals come more as a result of having an understanding and respect for the subject than simply having the technical expertise to operate a camera. Browsing through the pages of *Further Afield*, there can be no doubt that such a body of work is the result of a life spent in close contact with animals and the countryside, viewed with an intensely creative eye. Without such an artistic insight, many of the objects photographed in this book would have been overlooked. Most telling of all, are the keenly observed details of inanimate subjects that constantly surround us. The beautiful pictures of thongweed buttons, and the scallop shell lying on lichen encrusted rock are just two examples of the kind of details, which for those who have visited these habitats, will evoke a sense of reference and appropriateness. After all, how many visitors to a Hebridean beach are not tempted to take home an empty seashell or interesting piece of driftwood as a very personal memento of their visit? Whatever the habitat, we find these iconic details repeated throughout the book but despite its appeal, such imagery is rarely seen in print.

A compelling facet of *Further Afield*, is the humour frequently seen in so many of Polly's pictures; from goat kids captured as they play on a sheep's back, to ponies yawning in an almost human manner, or a black sheep

sporting a pure white beard of snow. Even a portrait of two totally different breeds of dog together, is filled with humour.

Another aspect that sets *Further Afield*, apart is the way in which many of the photographs have been composed to show both man-made and natural subjects together. All too often photographers are tempted to exclude all evidence of our impact on the landscape, yet for wildlife, the ruined buildings and drystane dykes in exposed locations like North Ronaldsay, must be some of the most secure places in which to shelter or raise young. Similarly, Polly is unafraid to venture out to photograph in inclement weather. The beautiful texture displayed in the coat of a rain-soaked red deer calf is just one example of the rewards available to those determined to try.

On the domestic front, I was at first surprised to read that most of Polly's canine subjects "pose beautifully". Photographing animals is like photographing children; there are inherent difficulties caused by the subjects' familiarity and desire to interact with the photographer with little or no warning. On reflection, I am certain Polly must have her own patient techniques borne from an empathy with the animals she obviously knows and loves. It is surprising just how wily seemingly tame animals can become when confronted with a human behaving abnormally. Just try pointing a camera at a blackface ewe with a lamb to appreciate how difficult it can be to get close. Unlikely as it may seem, the skills required are akin to those used by professional stalkers, and are certainly also needed for any form of wildlife photography. Clearly when looking at the sequence of seal photographs and many others in this book, these skills have richly paid off.

Photographing shy, captive birds of prey presents similar problems. Indeed, most professional nature photographers are tempted to work with captive raptors at some time, even if they don't always admit to doing so! Often, birds are hired for the purpose which raises the question that some of these might otherwise be flying free were it not for the commercial incentive to keep them. Reading Polly's stories, and looking at her pictures, this is not the situation here. There is an honesty about her approach, and it appears that most are held whilst in the process of being rehabilitated with the prospect of eventual release back into the wild. The choice of reading material shown in the amusing photograph on page 45, gives a clue to the very real commitment required when undertaking such a task. Few would be prepared to find the time to dedicate to such work, but I suspect that for Polly, it is both a priority and responsibility to do what comes naturally. I also hope she finds time to continue with her photography and writing. This is a delightfully unusual book, and I greatly look forward to seeing more of the same.

Laurie Campbell

Contents

1. Further Afield   *1*

2. Isles of the Forth   28

3. Birds of Prey   42

4. Winter   50

5. Meadow, Wood & Hedgerow   59

6. Domestic Front   77

7. North Ronaldsay   94

8. Grouse Encounter   111

9. Home Farm   114

Further Afield

Cleit, Village Bay, St Kilda

Village Bay, St Kilda

The magnificent St Kilda archipelago, Britain's furthest-flung outpost, lies approximately 110 miles due west of mainland Scotland. Reaching the islands is never easy as the Atlantic is fiercely erratic, and it takes approximately 8 hours by boat from North Uist. St Kilda's story is tragic yet intriguing. The islanders who originally survived on a diet based on gannets, puffins and fulmars, were evacuated in 1930, and now the maze of ruined cottages and cleits are all that remains of their extraordinary lives and unique culture. Hundreds of cleits dot Hirta, the main island, and were used to store the harvest of seabirds, turf and sheep. Photography was challenging due to heavy rain storms flying in off the Atlantic, and squally gusts of wind. As they cleared away leaving us soaked, the sun briefly broke through and momentarily picture taking was possible. I was fascinated by the cleits, the drama of the cliffs, the Soay sheep, the St Kilda wrens, and a beautiful browny-green seaweed on the jetty, *sea thong*, revealed by the exceptionally low tide.

The vast sea stacs, *Stac Lee* and *Stac an Armin*, are home to the world's largest gannetry, and as we travelled round the huge rock bastions and passed Boreray, I was overawed by one of the most dramatic wildlife extravaganzas to be seen anywhere in the British Isles. Scotland's wealth of islands, and remoter places have always drawn me magnetically and provide wonderful opportunities for photography, but as always time is the enemy.

Sea thong

3

Stac Lee, St Kilda

Stac Lee

Soay tup, St Kilda

Highland Home

Camus nan Geall, Ardnamurchan

Heavy traffic, Ardnamurchan

Abandoned, Luing

Easy care horse, Ardnamurchan

Stalking in Glenartney

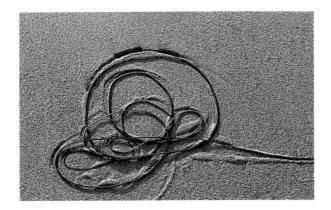

Weed patterns

Oystercatcher probe

Ben Resipol, Loch Sunart

Mill, Luing

Pine cones

Oak trees, Sound of Mull

Scallop shell

11

The Coo's lick

Gone with the wind

Cooling off

Old rope

Dead boat, Luing

Scallop shells

Dead boat, Berneray

14

Fowl play

At home in Tiree

Berneray

Cat leap

Ardtoe

Castle Tioram

Berneray

Shetland ponies

Another wet day in the Highlands

Lichen post

Lichen dyke

Mervyn Browne

South Country Cheviots

Shetland ewe and lamb

Blackface tups

Isles of the Forth

The Firth of Forth is home to two remarkably rich wildlife habitats – the tiny Isle of May, and the Bass Rock. During the spring and summer these two seabird havens are the breeding grounds of literally thousands of birds. On the Isle of May vast numbers of puffins return to breed, raising a single black fluffed chick in burrows round the island. In the early mornings and evenings huge flocks of puffins fill the sky as they throng in great wheels, while on the vertiginous cliffs, guillemots, razorbills and kittiwakes pack together in avian high rise accommodation. Fulmars and shags also breed here, and large numbers of eider ducks resemble round plum puddings as they sit tight on their eggs amongst sea campion and thrift. While walking round the island Arctic, common and Sandwich terns dive bomb with great intent, and the air is thick with the cries of hundreds of assorted gulls and oystercatchers. We have been fortunate to spend two summer holidays on the May and have been blessed with Mediterranean weather each time. Sometimes this part of the Forth coast can be swathed in thick sea haar, and of course wind on an exposed island such as this always hampers the photographer.

The Bass Rock, a vast volcanic plug steeped in history, has the largest North Atlantic gannet colony on the east coast of the British Isles, and holds approximately 10% of the world's population. With a wingspan of almost 2 metres, the gannet dives into the sea with great velocity catching fish sometimes as deep as thirty feet below the waves. With incredible adaptations to its skull and lungs, it is a miracle of wildlife engineering and one of the most fascinating of British birds.

Gannets pair for life and return to the same minute space where they bred previously. Here they will lay a single egg and rear a chick which they feed on regurgitated fish. Birds that overstep the boundaries between nests are reprimanded with harsh croaks and a stab from the incredibly powerful bill. During the winter months most of the birds travel south to the Bay of Biscay and the Mediterranean, and some even manage to reach the equator.

I only had a few hours on the Bass Rock and was totally overawed by the spectacle as literally thousands of jostling gannets crammed together busy with the breeding and feeding business. Some were amorously displaying to one another, offering pieces of dried weed and feathers as nest building material, while others stood high on the rocks raising their bills into the air in a courtship display called *skypointing*. Surrounded by photographic possibilities and with but one chance to capture the scene, I left this extraordinary place drunk with sea air and euphoria, satiated by all I had witnessed, covered in splashes of gannet guano, and desperately wishing that I could have spent days and days there in order to record it better.

The Bass Rock from Tantallon Castle

Isle of May - The Low Light, no longer used as a lighthouse but home of the island's Bird Observatory and our base while staying on the island.

The South Horn, Pilgrim's Haven

The Bass Rock Lighthouse

Pilgrim's Haven with Anstruther in the distance.

Isle of May - All that remains of Scotland's first manned light beacon built in 1636.

Gannets on the Bass Rock

Puffins

Herring gull

Shag

Kittiwakes

During my time on the May, I became obsessed with stalking the dozens of dozing grey seals that hauled out on to the barnacle and weed covered rocks. While their eyesight is in fact very poor, their sense of smell is acute so keeping the wind in the right direction is always important. I spend hours on my stomach crawling through pools and round rocks coming so close to my subjects that not only can I smell their fishy breath, but can also hear their grumbling and snarling as they tried to oust one another from a

particularly favoured rock. At one moment I was so busy photographing seals in front of me that I did not notice a youngster, lumbering over the rocks behind me. We played a cat and mouse game for some time before it finally winded me and fled into a warm pool.

Kittiwake chick

Razorbills

Puffins on watch duty

Kittiwake & chick

Shags are resident on the Isle of May throughout the year. When seen from a distance their plumage may appear drab and dull, however, when viewed up close in sunlight, it is a miracle of iridescent chequered patterning. With brilliant emerald green eye, the shag is a stunning bird, smaller and lighter in build than its close relative, the cormorant. Almost reptilian in appearance, the young shags sit on their nests of dried weed awaiting the return of the adults with food. As we passed beneath their nesting ledges, the dense covering of slimy weed and droppings made walking without falling well-nigh impossible. This treacherous surface was thereafter nicknamed, Shag Pile.

Angel Stack, Pilgrim's Haven

Birds of Prey

Kestrel

Chimney owlet

Tawny owlet

Buzzard

For many years I have been taking in injured birds of prey. While many are too badly damaged to be viable, the ones that do recover are very rewarding. My aim is to return them to the wild, but frequently their injuries are too severe and they have to be put down.

I have a seventeen year old tawny owl that became too tame. He paired up with another tawny we had in the aviaries and for several years they successfully reared a single chick which we released.

I receive more tawny owls than any other birds and have developed a particular passion for this supremely adapted owl which manages to thrive alongside man and all his developments. The tawny is a true survivor and often appears to have the will to recover. Each year we are brought orphan owlets and hack them out over the summer months. In the evenings they return for food filling the night sky with their hooting and shrieking. They frequently land on the open bedroom window sill in the middle of the night. Recently our efforts have been richly rewarded for a pair of hand-reared owls successfully nest in the chimney of the old bothy adjacent to the house. When the owlets emerge and sit blinking on the chimney top for the first time, the swallows and house martins dive bomb them making a great fuss about the intrusion.

In recent years, the osprey has made a come back after being close to the brink of extinction. Their growing number and success has meant that more meet with accidents and are injured, and subsequently a few are also brought to us.

Tawny owlets

Short-eared owl

Short-eared owl

Buzzard

Long-eared owl

Barn owl

Golden eaglet

Little owl

Peregrine

Osprey

Tawny owl

Buzzard chick

Osprey

Short-eared owl

Long-eared owl

Tawny owl

Winter

Birches, Glen Lyon

Hogweed stem

Sycamore key

Bracken

Giant hogweed

Beech masts

Frozen gate catch

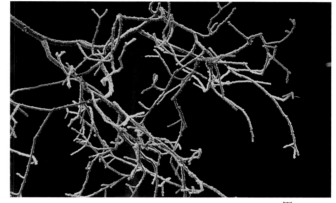

Tracery

Kenmore, Perthshire

Kinloch Rannoch

River Lyon

Oak

Sheep's wool

Roro, Glen Lyon

Birches

Early morning

Ice patterns

River Lyon

Schiehallion from Dunalastair, Perthshire

Broom

Meadow, Wood & Hedgerow

Ox-eye daisy

Oak

Beech

Oak

60

Oak leaves

Sycamore

Spanish Chestnut

Ash

62

Spanish Chestnut

Woodcock

Sitka spruce

Pine bark

Web

Reed mace

Larch

Larch wood

Heath grasses

Loch Monzievaird, Perthshire

Mare's tail

Frog

Hawkweed

Willowherb

Giant hogweed

Kestrel

Hawthorn

Poppies

Marsh orchid

Greater knapweed

Ox-eye daisy

Bracken frond

Foxgloves

Dandelion clock

Ferns

The Domestic Front

Straw dog

Bernese Mountain dogs

Border collie & Hungarian Viszla

Golden retrievers

Sophie & Lucy

For me life without a dog is unthinkable. My Border collie, Kim, turned up on our doorstep one wild winter's night with a piece of string round her neck. Despite endless telephone calls no one came to claim her. She was so sweet natured and affectionate that I prayed no one would. Eventually a Land Rover drove up the drive and the owner appeared and told me that he was having terrible trouble training her. Though I tried to buy the collie, he was intent on trying again, and took her away cowering in the back. He told me that if he failed to train her then I might have her. Over the next few months she was seen wandering round the neighbourhood. Clearly she and her owner were very incompatible. I rang him one evening and found that he was at his wit's end, "she's totally useless", he told me. I grabbed a bottle of whisky from the cupboard and leapt into the car, handing it over in exchange for one extremely timorous collie. The gamble paid off and within weeks I found I had the easiest and most obediently loyal dog I have ever had the pleasure to own. And quite the best outcome from any bottle of whisky.

I love to photograph animals of all kinds, but dogs are usually the best subjects as most of them pose beautifully. As I travel round the countryside I become very attached to some of my subjects. Rab and Sandy, two Scottie brothers, are tremendous characters, always pleased to see me. Then there is Skip, a bearded collie who is most at home in his owner's beaten up old vehicles. His hilarious innocent expression and blinking eyes after he has committed his crimes of destruction, including the total demolition of his owner's gear stick and steering wheel, as well as his picnics, just make everyone more fond of him.

People become more bonded to their dogs than almost any other animal and their all too short lives leave great voids behind. There are obviously many who have a preference for cats, but I find them far harder to photograph as they have independent natures and often will not oblige. I have been asked to photograph a few polecats and ferrets. They are almost impossible to capture on film except when asleep, since their constant frenetic movement just leaves me with far too many blurred shots.

I sometimes go to an animal welfare centre to photograph the inmates for use on a calendar. The hardest part of these visits is returning alone as so many of the dogs and cats, puppies and kittens are awaiting a good new home, and in many cases have been abysmally treated.On these occasions I admit to having a real problem of self-control, especially when the faces look at me as I endeavour unsuccessfully to turn a blind eye.

While photographing animals some unusual pictures can emerge. When I went to photograph Jolly, a Staffordshire bull terrier, for a feature on the breed, I also ended up photographing his partner in crime, Sandy, a very lovable, wiry little terrier with a penchant for ratting and rabbiting. Despite his love of the chase, his nervousness and fear of the family's pet hen was most amusing and when the hen shared the sofa with the boys, the bird was definitely in control.While Sandy was most certainly henpecked, Jolly and the hen were quite laid back about one another. Like humans, dogs vary in character enormously.

Labrador puppies

81

Henpecked

At ease with the situation

Rab & Sandy

Sienna

Golden retriever

Life`s a beach

Logging out

The final straw

SSPCA cats

A healthy diet is important

Polecat ferret

Christmas is so exhausting

Kim

Kim

Sienna & roe fawn

Skip - road dog

Kim

Sandy

Hattie

North Ronaldsay

Like tattoos, places and happenings leave their indelible mark. There are few places so etched on my mind as Orkney's northernmost island, North Ronaldsay. This low-lying, fertile island is largely governed by tide and weather, and is now serviced regularly by a subsidised, small islander aircraft, which allows people to travel to and fro for an unbelievably reasonable sum of money. The day we flew to the island the sea was a glorious turquoise blue, and the landscape below a magical patchwork of striped fields, meandering dry stone dykes, and shorelines fringed with emerald green weed and white sandy beaches.

North Ronaldsay is famous for its extraordinary primitive sheep. This small, ancient, wiry breed, a member of the northern group of short-tailed sheep, has evolved to exist on a diet that is almost entirely based on seaweed. The sheep are kept on the seashore by the longest continuous stretch of dry stone wall in the world. Approximately 12 miles of dyke surround the island's coast and is Grade A listed – as important as historic buildings such as Edinburgh Castle, or the magnificent St Magnus Cathedral in Kirkwall.

The life of a North Ronaldsay sheep is strictly governed by the sea. As soon as the tide begins to turn, there is the sound of hooves on rock as troops of sheep skip down to the tide-line in search of their favourite seaweeds, dulse and laminaria. As the skerries are uncovered, many venture far out to feed. There are approximately 2500 sheep on North Ronaldsay, and it is pressures of life on the beach that have largely created the breed. The tups and wethers (castrated males) are kept on the shore throughout the year, but the ewes are brought into the crofts and in-bye ground in the spring to lamb. Here they remain until August when they go back on to the shore for the autumn and winter. Usually a ewe will only rear a single lamb. The second lamb in a set of twins will frequently be humanely culled at birth as with such a harsh environment one strong lamb has a far greater chance of survival over the wild winter months. The sheep are rounded up in *pundings* when many of their owners work together to bring a particular group of animals in to stone built fanks, or *punds*. The incredible agility and cleverness of the sheep frequently leaves the handlers battered and bruised. With wild natures, some flighty sheep leap madly into the air sending their captors flying as they slip on the rocks ending up soaked and defeated. Some sheep evade capture altogether by swimming out to sea. North Ronaldsay sheep are far from stupid.

Traditionally the wethers were culled around Christmas time when they had grown fat from the large amounts of seaweed driven ashore by the winter gales. Now they are sent away to the abattoir when they are between 3-5 years old depending on their size, and the more mature meat produced is supremely delicious, low in cholesterol and fat free.

Every day at the turning of the tide, I sat on the rocks and watched the extraordinary spectacle as the small, lithe, multi-coloured sheep agilely leapt over the large numbers of dozing seals on the rocks. The seals remained unconcerned. Some looked up, opened one eye, groaned a little then returned to their slumbers, while others did not even move. After the sheep had filled themselves with great fronds of shining weed, some returned and lay amid the seals, to cud. I found the sunbathing seals far easier to approach than the sheep, although after a week meeting many of the

same ones every day, they began to ignore me as I approached them and took photographs.

The island's unique sheep management is organised by the Sheep Court. Originally based on its six crofting townships, this ancient system used to have two representatives from each township with the laird as the chairman. Today the sheep are managed as a communal flock with all sheep owner's making decisions. The dyke involves continual maintenance as large sections are frequently undermined by the battering of the sea and the incessant winter gales. With North Ronaldsay's dwindling population, finding enough man power to keep up with the wall repair is an increasing problem.

Behind the dyke, huge beds of yellow flag iris sprawl eternally and above them in summer snipe drum tirelessly overhead in territorial displays, while terns and gulls wheel and shriek. The ground is studded with carpets of orchids and marsh marigolds, and round the freshwater pools, oystercatchers, curlews, redshank, mallard and teal rear their young. This is also the stopping off point for thousands of migrants, and many rarities are ringed and recorded, caught temporarily in the special purpose-built nets.

In June the common seals give birth to their pups. Several times I came across mothers with their new babies, and took pictures from a safe distance. Seals do not hesitate to put you firmly in your place if you venture too close, and are fiercely protective of their offspring particularly in the first few hours after their birth.

The Beach Boys

Fulmar

North Ronaldsay's first lighthouse at Dennisness

North Ronaldsay's first lighthouse was built in 1789, and was one of the first four to be constructed by the Northern Lighthouse Board. Now redundant, it occasionally houses a pair of nesting ravens on its window ledge. The new tower was built in 1854 and automated in 1998. This is Britain's tallest land built lighthouse and has 176 steps. The long climb up to the top was well worth it to admire the view of the longest stretch of continuous dyke. The island panorama was outstanding even though it was too hazy to take clear pictures. Circular dyked enclosures called *plantie cruzs*, are also clearly visible from the top of the lighthouse. These were built by the people of North Ronaldsay to protect their vegetables and seed from both the sheep and the weather.

Fulmars nest all around the island, often close up to the ancient walls, or on the plantie cruzs. Their large dark eyes, and extraordinary tube-nose bills give them a somewhat soft appearance, belying the fact that they will spit a foul smelling oil all over anyone that threatens them.

The new lighthouse & plantie cruz

Marsh marigolds

Marsh orchids

Mallard

Fulmar

Mare's tail

Flag iris

Starlings & rabbit

Redshank

Common seal

Grouse Encounter

The red grouse is fiercely territorial. Occasionally, members of the grouse family become so obsessed with protecting their patch that they lose all fear of man and will attack intruders what ever their size.

We came across this militant cock grouse in a remote Perthshire glen. He was posing by the roadside and when we stopped to take pictures, he launched his first attack. Our first encounter with him left us in no doubt as to who was in charge, and his total aversion to passing mountain bikers, left me reeling with laughter. As their brightly clad forms swathed in psychedelic lycra shot by, the grouse hurled himself at them like a supersonic bullet. Although his target was missed, his intentions were plain to see. Showing absolutely no fear of passing cars, he flung himself at them too. Competing with such large opposition I felt he had little chance of survival.

We returned to look for the Lord of the Moor one beautiful day towards the end of summer, and found him in almost the same place where we had first met. While I took pictures of this remarkably stunning little bird, wildlife artist Keith Brockie, enjoyed a particularly close encounter.

Of course retaliation from Keith was not part of the game. However, he chose to stay a while to take all the abuse that the small bird was hurling at him. The densely feathered feet inflicted some large scratches while the call, *go back, go back, go back* seemed very pertinent. After a while the victor strode off into the heather, triumphantly grumbling to himself.

Home Farm

Freddy & Onslow

115

The pictures in *Home Farm*, are of many of our own animals and birds. Animals that know you are easier to photograph, although some of ours are so friendly that they rush up too close to the lens, steaming it up with their breath. I have had a passion for sheep since I had my first blackface pet lamb, Lulu, when we lived in Ardnamurchan. Though we no longer farm commercially, I will always keep a small mixed flock purely as a hobby because I enjoy working with them. They make brilliant photographic subjects and earn more from the pictures I take of them than from agricultural ventures at this time. Sadly farming has changed so much in recent years and it is well-nigh impossible to make a living off a small farm. New rules and regulations have become a terrible mine field, and waste precious time that should be spent with the stock.

All our sheep have very distinctive characters. When we had a large flock, I always had several pets. One mule called Myrtle, gave birth to 7 sets of triplets and was put down at the ripe old age of fourteen, while Bean cost £3 in the market and also had a great many lambs.

We have a few old-fashioned coloured Shetlands which people are surprised to find are highly intelligent.I went to the local rare breeds sale and could not find a Shetland tup that I liked. Just as I was about to give up and go home, a man walked in with an attractive small, moorit-coloured tup on a halter. He was exactly what I was looking for. When I brought the tup home it was still too early to put him out with the ewes. Instead he spent hours standing on a large rock in his field surveying them regally, obviously eyeing-up the talent. He looked far more like a wild moufflon than a British native breed. One glorious autumn morning he was particularly dramatic and I rushed up with the camera. The Golden Fleece pictures were the result.

Bramble, a mule, has also had many lambs and her broad back is clearly an attraction to both our goats and her own offspring as they like to lie or play on it. Tilly, the blackface ewe below, came from Glenartney in a remote part of Perthshire.

Hens also make great subjects and have very varied characters although are seldom credited with much intelligence. The large exhibition Rhode Island Red cockerel in this chapter is magnificent during the breeding season and looks after his wives very attentively. Unfortunately, though they are a most attractive breed, their laying capabilities are extremely poor.

Tilly

Ho! Ho! Ho!

The Golden Fleece

120

Acting the goat

Goats are real characters and love human company. We have a family group of six African pygmy goats and they provide us with great entertainment as their antics are often hilarious.

Before the new livestock transportation restrictions, they frequently came in the car with us, and also enjoyed long walks with the dogs. Two of them appeared in a school nativity play appearing on stage decked in tinsel amid adoring shepherds, kings, and Mary and Joseph. They behaved impeccably and even bleated at the right moments. However at the end of their performance, I noticed that one of them had done a very good job giving one of the young shepherds a haircut. Luckily, his hair was rather long and he did not notice the pieces lying on the floor.

One morning I went out to feed the sheep and found that two of the goat kids were using the broad backs of the sheep as a trampoline. I rushed inside to fetch the camera and managed to capture some pictures of their escapades. That afternoon, the ewes were clipped. The following morning I watched as the goat kids leapt back up on to one fat ewe's back, only to discover that without the dense wool, staying on board was totally impossible.

123

Few could resist the charms of a new born roe fawn and all too frequently fawns are unwittingly picked up by well-wishers who think that they have been abandoned. It is always an awful feeling when we receive a fawn that we know perfectly well was merely lying up waiting for its mother to return, and people never seem to be able to remember exactly where they were found. But Rosie was found lying next to her dead mother on the road and brought to us when she was only about a week old. Deer are highly nervous creatures and hand-rearing them is not always simple. Some will take to a bottle straight away, while others are just not interested, suffering acutely from stress and fear. She turned out to be one of the most difficult orphans I have ever dealt with as she

refused to suckle at all, and would not even take milk from a bowl. All the vegetables and leaves that we offered her, the coarse mix and chopped apples, were also shunned. Nothing would tempt her and she soon became ill and listless. Watching such a perfect little creature going downhill is dreadful however tough you are.

I had purposefully kept our bearded collie, Berry away from her trying to ensure that the depressed animal had no further stress to contend with. Just as I was reaching the end of my tether after another failed feeding attempt, and had accepted the fact that I was shortly going to be losing her, the collie burst in and started to lick all the spilt milk off her coat. The result was dramatic. The fawn started to squeak in obvious pleasure, while the dog licked her all over, pushing her coat up into little waves with her tongue. From that point on the situation changed, and Rosie who had been hanging on to a thread, took on a new lease of life. The dog though became rather more neurotic than usual, and went off her food for a while preferring to share the vegetarian diet of the fawn.

That summer, Berry spent most of her time with her new baby and after our walks would rush back to the paddock to find her. They played wonderfully carefree games chasing one another round and round the field, eventually collapsing exhausted together for a sleep.

Rosie is still with us and lives contentedly with the sheep and goats. She is tame with us and unafraid by our dogs, but strangers and their dogs are a different matter. She is not easy to treat when sick as she puts on the fiercest of struggles when given any form of medication. We had to treat her for pneumonia several years ago and even the vet was surprised by her strength. Her sharp stiletto hooves have inflicted me with some dramatic bruises over the years we have had her, and I always dread having to give her an injection. Every summer she is visited by a roe buck. However, she is only about two-thirds the size of an adult roe doe, and we are sure that this is the reason why she has never had a fawn.

131

The Last Laugh